The Wide World of Girl Guiding and Girl Scouting

Girl Scouts of the U.S.A.

830 Third Avenue
New York, N.Y. 10022

 GIRL SCOUTS OF THE U.S.A.

Mrs. Orville L. Freeman, *President*
Frances Hesselbein, *National Executive Director*

Inquiries related to
The Wide World of
Girl Guiding and Girl Scouting
should be addressed to
Program,
Girl Scouts of the U.S.A.,
830 Third Avenue,
New York, N. Y. 10022

Copyright 1980 by
Girl Scouts of the United States of America

All rights reserved

First Impression 1980

Printed in the United States of America

ISBN 0-88441-143-5
Girl Scout Catalog No. 19-713

10   9   8   7   6

Table of Contents

"Look wide! And when you think you are looking wide, look wider still."

— *Lord Baden-Powell*

Introduction

You are part of a family of more than eight million Girl Guides and Girl Scouts who live in about 100 countries spread out all over the world. Imagine visiting members of this large family.

You'd play their games and help them cook their favorite foods. You'd sing the songs they love and make their arts and crafts. You'd learn about exciting Girl Guide/Girl Scout activities and share their pride in their nation. You'd become a friend.

This book gives you the chance to learn about and do some of the things your Girl Scout family around the world does. Have fun reading about Ghana, Greece, India, Kenya, Mexico, Peru, the Philippines and becoming friends with your sisters there.

But, before visiting with these Girl Guides/Girl Scouts, you can take a trip to the four homes shared by our big family. These are the four world centers which belong to the World Association of Girl Guides and Girl Scouts (WAGGGS).

Almost in the center of the Western Hemisphere in Mexico is **Our Cabaña.** Many Senior Girl Scouts and adults from North, Central, and South America and the Caribbean travel to Our Cabaña to enjoy the beauty of Mexico and to meet Girl Guides and Girl Scouts who come from all over the world. You can try Mexican folk arts in the crafts center; swim in Our Cabaña's pool; learn about the flowers, trees, and cacti on the grounds; and climb a nearby pyramid built centuries ago by Aztec Indians.

The next stop is London, England. **Olave House,** our center there, is surrounded by the bustle of a capital city with an exciting past. At Olave House, you are sure to meet other Girl Guides/Girl Scouts from every part of the world who will be staying there. Take time out from sightseeing to share a true English tea with them in the garden at Olave House. (Olave House will be closed for approximately two years, beginning September 30, 1988. It will be replaced by a new Olave House, which will be located at the Olave Center on Lyndhurst Road, London, and is expected to be ready for occupancy late in 1990.)

Now, on to Switzerland and **Our Chalet.** Summer days there can be spent hiking and picnicking among beautiful mountains and flower-filled meadows. Go in the winter and you may ski or toboggan. At night, you and all your Girl Guide/Girl Scout friends will gather around the big fireplace to sing favorite songs from all over the world.

Are you ready for a big adventure in the middle of Asia? There in India, near Bombay, is our newest center, **Sangam.** Help harvest bananas, sugarcane, peanuts, and vegetables growing right at the center. You might eat an Indian dinner served on a giant leaf.

On your visit, you could go to an Indian festival with an Indian family, play games with Indian children, see the ancient Ajanta and Ellora caves with their paintings and temples, visit wildlife and bird refuges. Do all these things with the Asian Girl Guides and Girl Scouts who visit Sangam often, and with girls from other parts of the world too. Like all the other world centers, Sangam is a wonderful place for making friends with Girl Guides and Girl Scouts.

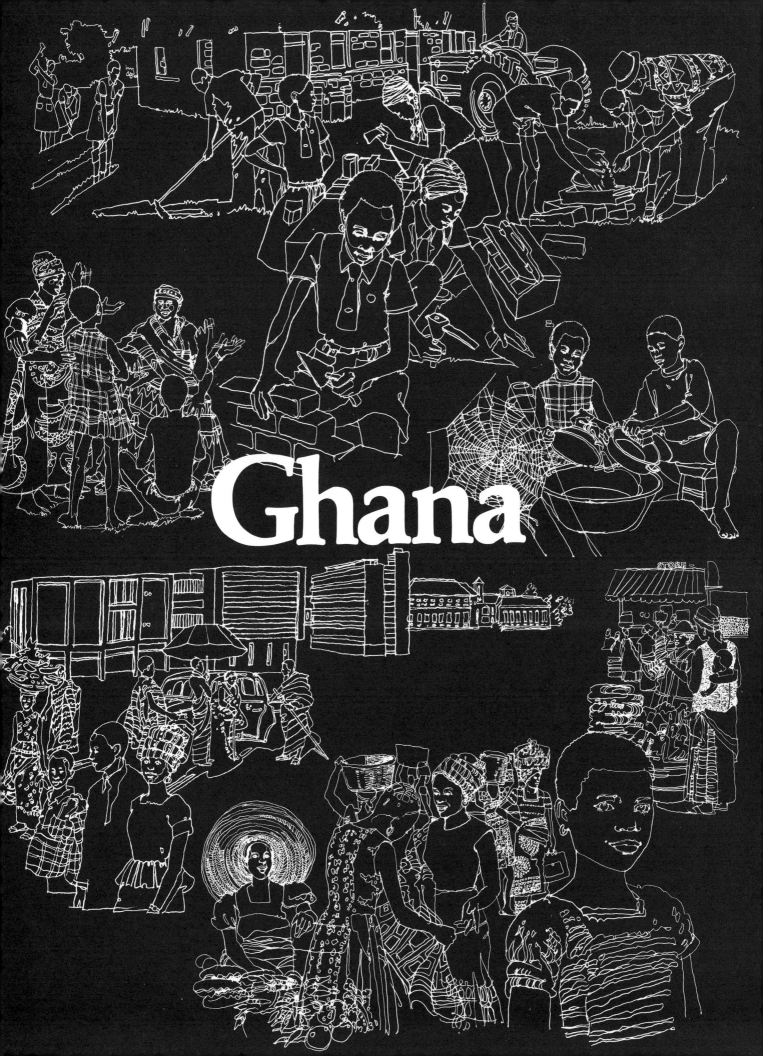

Ghana

The next time you bite into your favorite chocolate bar, close your eyes and imagine a warm, sunny land of thick, green forests, wide open grasslands, and great rivers. This is Ghana, a country on the west coast of Africa. Here farmers grow and harvest more cocoa beans than any other country in the world. From these beans (or seeds), we get chocolate. In addition to farming, people in Ghana fish and work in mines and factories. They live in small towns and cities.

Over 1,500 years ago, Ghana was one of several African empires in West Africa. The rulers of these ancient empires traded salt, gold, lumber, and hides with Arabs and Europeans. Visitors to West Africa in the 1400s were impressed by the wealth and learning they found there, and by the complex governments.

Since justice was important to West Africans, the country was very safe for travelers and for the people who lived there.

Like most great empires Ghana didn't last forever. At the end of the 1500s there was fighting among the peoples in West Africa. This weakened the area and Europeans began to conquer African countries. Great Britain ruled Ghana for over 100 years. The British called this land the Gold Coast because there was much gold there. In 1957 Ghana won its independence from Great Britain.

The people wanted an African name for their nation and chose the name Ghana after the ancient empire.

Ghana is well known for its businesswomen who run the outdoor markets. In Ghana and throughout Africa, people bring the crafts they make and the food they grow to the marketplaces in towns and cities. If you walked through the market-place, you wouldn't see price tags on the rice, the bananas, or the yams. Instead of paying a set price, you would bargain with a merchant until you agreed on a price that seemed fair to both of you. Chances are you'd be bargaining with a woman who learned her trade as a young girl.

One of the most important crafts in Ghana is designing and weaving special fabrics called *Kente cloth*. *Kente* designs have become so popular that they are copied by fashion designers in many parts of the world, including the United States. You can design your own cloth by weaving and/or tie-dyeing, just like the Ghanaians do.

There are many ways to tie-dye to make colorful patterns on a cloth. One of the easiest ways is to tie small tight knots with string in an old sheet. Then dip the sheet into a pail of dye. The longer you leave the sheet in the dye, the darker the color will be. Rinse the sheet twice in cold water and hang it up to dry. When your sheet is dry, untie the knots. You will find the dye didn't reach where you tied tight knots. This will make your pattern. You may want to have your own outdoor market to display your fabrics.

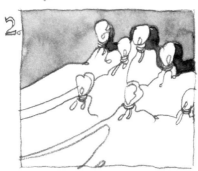

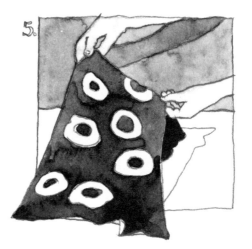

People in many parts of Africa don't eat much meat, especially beef. This is because there is an insect in Africa that makes cattle sick. Chicken is a popular meat, and other sources of protein are peanuts and beans. Here is a Ghanaian recipe.

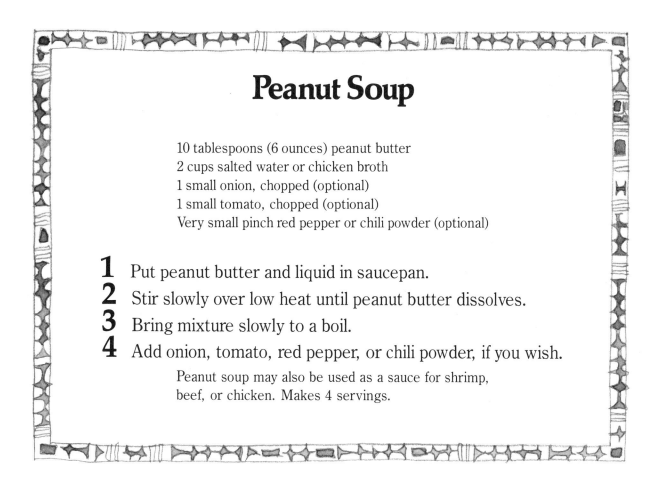

Peanut Soup

10 tablespoons (6 ounces) peanut butter
2 cups salted water or chicken broth
1 small onion, chopped (optional)
1 small tomato, chopped (optional)
Very small pinch red pepper or chili powder (optional)

1 Put peanut butter and liquid in saucepan.

2 Stir slowly over low heat until peanut butter dissolves.

3 Bring mixture slowly to a boil.

4 Add onion, tomato, red pepper, or chili powder, if you wish.

Peanut soup may also be used as a sauce for shrimp, beef, or chicken. Makes 4 servings.

Ghana Girl Guides Association

Girl Guiding started in Ghana back in 1921. Today, the Ghana Girl Guides Association has about 6,000 members. Girls ages 7 to 10 are Ananse Guides. They are named after Ananse, the spider who is a hero of many famous folk tales. He is thought to be wise, clever, and good. Here is the Ananse Guide story.

Once upon a time, in the middle of a forest, stood a little house under an oil palm tree. Inside the house lived a grandmother and two lively grandchildren. The children were twins, so, according to the custom, they had the same name. They were called Abena One and Abena Two.

Every day, when Abena One and Abena Two went off to school, grandmother would walk to the farm and dig and hoe and gather a little food to bring home and cook for the children. But sometimes she felt tired and weak and couldn't bring too much food.

One day, when Abena One and Abena Two came home from school, they saw grandmother sitting by the big cooking pot, but the pot was empty! Grandmother looked at the children sadly. "I have worked hard," she said, "but now my back is too bent and my arms are too weak. I can't dig and cut as I used to. Unless I get new arms and a new back, I can't bring home food anymore."

That night the children lay awake for a long time. Finally, when they knew their grandmother was asleep, they tiptoed out of the house. "Abena One," said Abena Two, "we must find our grandmother a new back!" "Abena Two," said Abena One, "we must find our grandmother new arms. Let's go and find a Wise One who can tell us what to do."

Soon they came upon a clearing where there was a little house. From inside they could hear a high, squeaky voice and a low, squeaky voice singing together:

Here they come, come one, come two,
What's the good they want to do?

The children went up to the door and peered in. There, sitting on two big logs, were two people with so many hands and so many feet that the children knew at once they must be Ananse and his wife.

Ananse waved the children in with two of his hands, pulled up two chairs with two more hands, and set two more mugs on the table with two more hands. His wife took cakes from the shelf with two hands and put them on mats with two more hands.

The children sat on the chairs. They were a little afraid. Then Ananse and his wife asked what they wanted. Abena One and Abena Two explained that their grandmother needed a strong new back and new arms.

Ananse and his wife listened quietly. They folded two of their arms on the table, scratched their heads with two more, and patted the children with two more.

Then Ananse's wife spoke. "My husband is very clever," she said, "but even the great Ananse cannot give new backs and new arms. But I will tell you a secret. The Good God has already sent your grandmother a new back and new arms. We will show them to you."

Ananse and his wife led the two children outside. "Close your eyes," Ananse said. Then Ananse led Abena One around the yard and put her hands on the back of _____. Abena One said, "That's a fine, strong back for my grandmother."

Then Ananse took Abena Two and led him around the yard and put his hands on the arms of _____. Abena Two said, "Those are fine, strong arms for my grandmother."

15

Ghana

Suddenly, there was a clap of thunder and both children opened their eyes. There they were, standing in the moonlight, holding on to each other. Ananse, his wife, and the little house had disappeared. The children laughed and then ran home quickly to their own house.

The next morning, they woke up very early and went out to the farm. They found a few plantains (bananas) and peppers and headed home. Then they swept the yard, gathered sticks, lit the fire, and cooked the food. Soon their grandmother awoke. She looked around in amazement. The children laughed and told her about their visit to Ananse. "Now we have enough strong backs and enough strong arms for all of us," they said. Their grandmother cried for joy.

Every day after that, the children worked hard on the farm before and after school. Soon they had the best farm in the village. They kept their house clean and neat, except for one little corner by the back door. For there, clinging to the doorpost by his many hands, was a small spider who looked very much like Ananse, and next to him another spider who looked very much like Ananse's wife.

16

Ananse Guides enjoy camping and paying visits to hospitals. In the villages where drinking water comes from public pipes or streams, Ananse Guides fetch water and balance the water bucket on their heads — without hands — all the way home! Try it — out-of-doors, of course! You'll soon see why girls in Ghana walk so gracefully.

Girls ages 10 to 14, who are Girl Guides, and girls 14 to 21, who

are Ranger Guides, all work hard to help their country become stronger. The government wants the people of Ghana to grow enough food for everyone in the country. So they started a program called Operation Feed Yourself to encourage people to plant vegetable gardens. The Ranger Guides help by holding work camps where they plant gardens, and by harvesting crops with farmers. Sometimes Girl Guides and Girl Scouts from several countries, including the United States, have joined their sister Guides in Ghana at their work camps. The Girl Guides also help build schools and clinics, and they help teach people to read.

Promise

I promise that I will do my best:
To do my duty to God,
To serve my Country and help other people,
And to keep the Guide Law.

English is the language used by the Girl
Guides of Ghana, so they use that language
for their Promise.

Uniform
Blue dress
Red tie
Brown belt

Girl Guide Pin
Blue trefoil on silver background

Ananse Pin
Silver spider and web

Greece

In Greece today, people live in modern cities, like Athens, or in small villages near the sea or in the mountains. Some of the people live on the more than 1,400 islands which are part of this country.

The mountains make farming difficult, but grapes, olives, citrus fruits, and some vegetables grow well because of the warm, sunny weather. Stylish clothes and fabrics are made in Greece. Shipping and fishing are also important, as they have been for hundreds of years.

Important parts of the history and way of life of the people in Europe, the Middle East, and the Western Hemisphere come from ancient Greece. Greek people created a world of arts and architecture. Their poems, myths, and stories are still translated into many languages and read today.

Greece had a system of laws and justice that makes us think of it as the birthplace of democracy. In fact, the word "democracy" comes from two Greek words: *demos*, meaning "the people," and *kratos*, meaning "authority." Democracy means authority of the people.

The ancient Greeks built beautiful temples with rows of lovely stone columns. The most famous of these temples, the Parthenon, is located on the Acropolis in Athens. *Acro polis* means "high city." On this hill within the city are found other important examples of Greek architecture, too. Buildings in many countries use the famous Greek columns. See if any buildings or houses in your area have Greek columns.

Music and dance are an important part of life in Greece today as in the past. Holidays, festivals, and almost any occasion call for singing and dancing. Many of these holidays and festivals are religious ones, showing the deep feeling the people have for the Greek Orthodox Church. One holiday, the Feast of Saint Basil, is celebrated on New Year's Day.

Saint Basil was an important founder of the Greek Orthodox Church. On this day, Greek families exchange gifts. In some parts of Greece, they celebrate with singing and dancing. Here is one of their songs for you to try.

Saint Basil

Moderato

Saint Ba-sil comes and pass-es by, And scorns us for no rea-son why; He comes from Cae-sa-re-a town. Mis-tress, bring, mis-tress, bring us some-thing down.

A new month's eve, a New Year's Eve,
Sweet rosemary, I beg your leave;
Joy be your lot the whole year round,
May your house be holy ground.

Did you know that Greece is the birthplace of the Olympics? They are named for athletic contests which were held in the valley of Olympia, near the city of Pirgos, starting in 776 B.C. That's nearly 3,000 years ago!

Today, the Olympic Games are held every four years in different cities of the world. Athletes from almost every country in the world compete in winter and summer sports. Perhaps you have seen the games on television.

At the Olympics, the athletes from Greece always march in first, to honor Greece as the home of the first Olympic Games. Relay runners bring a lighted torch all the way from the ancient valley of Olympia to light the Olympic flame. This signifies the start of the games.

Your troop can get together with some other troops and have your own games. Decide which sports you will play. They can be both individual sports (running, skating) and team sports (soccer, softball), just like the official Olympics. You might make medals to award to the winners. If you like, different troops can represent different countries, and afterward everyone can celebrate with an international festival.

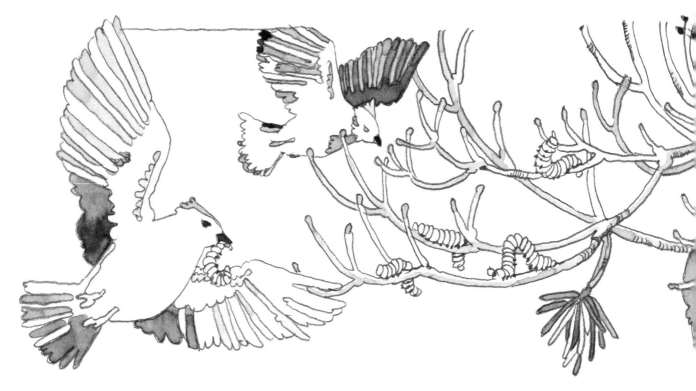

Soma Hellinidon Odigon
Girl Guides of Greece

In Greece, Girl Guides are known as Odigoi. Girls ages 6 to 11 are Poulia (Birds). Like Brownies everywhere, Poulia have their own story. It is a fable like Aesop's fables. Aesop was a storyteller who lived in Greece thousands of years ago.

After you read the Pouli story, you may want to make drawings to go with it, act it out, or have a puppet show to share the story with others. You could read and act out some of the Aesop fables, too. Here is the Pouli story.

Once there was a large forest. Many animals lived in the forest — big animals like foxes and deer, and little animals, especially birds.

One day, the pine trees started to shed their needles, until, day after day, little by little, all the branches of all the trees became bare. The big animals were frightened because now they would not be protected from the rain, the wind, and the snow. Many animals moved to another forest.

Then a wise old bird called the other birds together and said, "We don't need to leave. We can save our forest. It's the caterpillars that are destroying the pine needles. So we will eat all the caterpillars."

The little birds got busy and ate and ate until they were quite full. But they didn't stop until all the caterpillars were gone. Then the pine needles started to grow again and all the animals came back to the forest.

The moral of this fable is: As little birds can save a whole forest, so girls can do a lot by helping others. The Pouli motto is *Dosse Kheri* (Give a Hand).

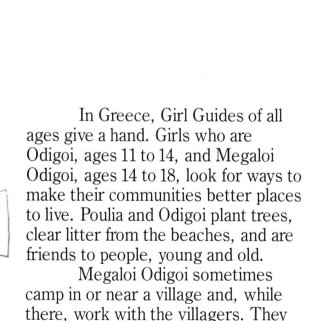

In Greece, Girl Guides of all ages give a hand. Girls who are Odigoi, ages 11 to 14, and Megaloi Odigoi, ages 14 to 18, look for ways to make their communities better places to live. Poulia and Odigoi plant trees, clear litter from the beaches, and are friends to people, young and old.

Megaloi Odigoi sometimes camp in or near a village and, while there, work with the villagers. They may clean and paint the town; teach songs, games, and good nutrition to the children; help to care for infants; or entertain with puppet shows. Sometimes, Senior Girl Scouts from other countries join in these summer service camps.

Iposhessi

Ipóshome stin timí mou ná prospathísso:
Ná káno to kathíkon mou prós tón Theó ké tín Patrída,
Ná voïthó ólous pantoú ké pántote,
Ná ipakoúo stón Nómo tís Odigoú.

Promise

I promise on my honor to try:
To do my duty to God and to my Country,
To help everybody, always and everywhere,
To obey the Law of the Guides.

Uniform
Light blue blouse
Dark green skirt
Brown-and-white striped tie

Girl Guide Pin
Black trefoil on gold background

Pouli Pin
Brown bird

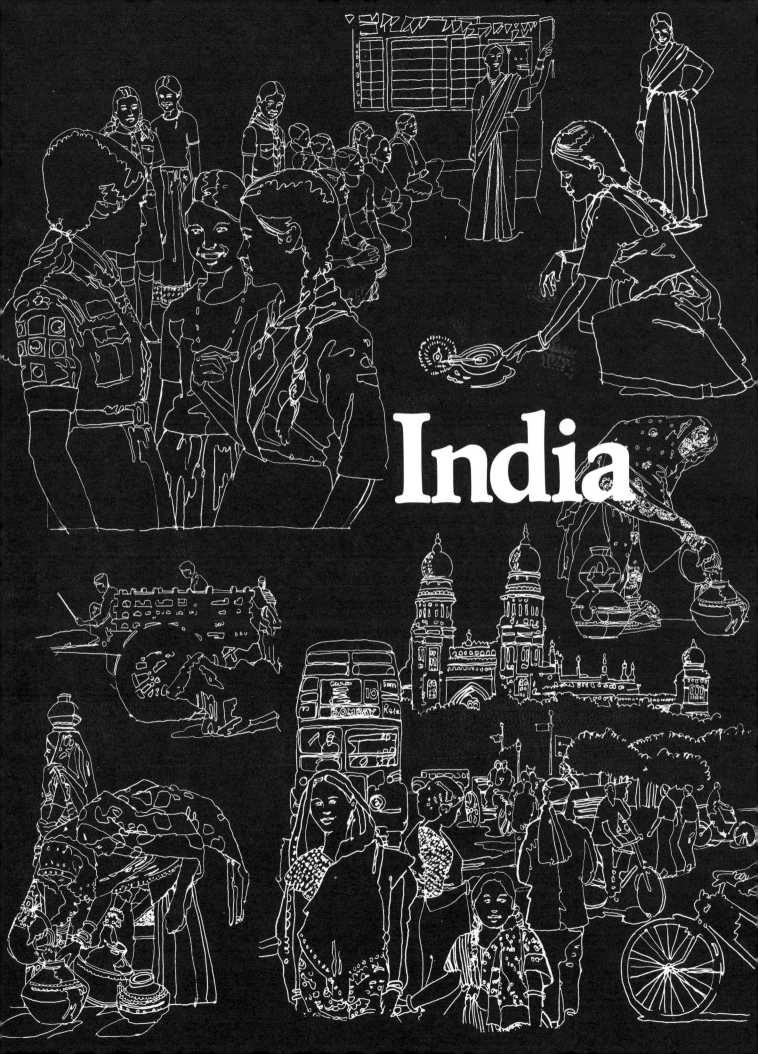

India

India is a country where you can get soaked in a monsoon, which is a season of heavy rain, at the same time someone else is trying to find a drink of water in a desert. It's a country that delights mountain lovers because it has the Himalayas, the highest mountains in the world.

Imagine walking down a street and hearing over ten different languages. Although Hindi is the official Indian language, 13 others are recognized as main languages. Many religions are important in India. Most Indians are Hindus, but there are also many Moslems, Christians, and Sikhs. A small number of Jewish people and Buddhists live in India today. India is the birthplace of the Buddhist religion.

India has an important place in today's world. It has a long, rich history and many ancient customs.

A favorite Indian holiday is the Hindu Festival of Lights, *Diwali*. It is

celebrated in October or November, in honor of Lakshmi, goddess of wealth. The day begins with a special *Diwali* breakfast. Later there are fireworks, bands, and processions carrying Lakshmi's image. When darkness comes, *Diwali* lamps are lit along the edges of roofs to attract Lakshmi's blessing. Another evening custom is for girls to float their lights across a nearby river. If a girl's *Diwali* lamp reaches the other shore still lit, her family will have good fortune for the next year.

Diwali lamps are small earthenware bowls which contain some oil and a wick. To make a *Diwali* lamp, you will need:

- Clay
- Small piece of string for wick
- Salad oil

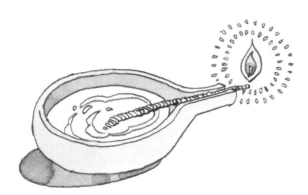

1 Roll the clay into a 5 cm (2 in.) ball.

2 Shape the clay into a bowl.

3 Add a lip to the bowl like a pouring spout to hold the wick.

4 Let the clay dry.

5 Put your wick in the wick holder.

6 Pour a little salad oil into the bowl.

7 When you are ready, light your lamp.

Indians live in big cities and villages. Bombay, the nearest large city to our world center, Sangam, is a great seaport and manufacturing city where everything from movies to steel is made. Indians in Bombay ride modern double-decker buses. They also travel on bicycles or motor scooters. A bicycle is inexpensive and saves fuel.

Riding a bicycle in an Indian city like Bombay, New Delhi, Calcutta, or Madras is a challenge. A bicyclist must watch out for carriages pulled by ponies, slow moving ox carts hauling farm produce, hundreds of other bicyclists, as well as buses, trucks, and cars. In very dry parts of India, bicyclists also have to steer around camel carts. Try setting up a bicycle course that might be similar to riding in an Indian city. (See pages 102 and 103 of *Worlds to Explore* for ideas.)

Many people in India are farmers and live in villages. The farmers raise buffalo cows, rice or wheat, vegetables, and fruits. Cows are very important in India because their milk is a good source of vitamins and protein for the Indians who do not eat meat. A buffalo cow gives very rich, delicious milk.

Many Indians, particularly Hindus, do not eat meat for religious reasons. Instead, they fix vegetables in interesting and appetizing ways.

Using the many spices that grow in their country, Indians make vegetable curries. Curry is a blend of spices. Here is a vegetable curry for you to try.

String Bean Curry

1 pound fresh string beans
1 large onion, chopped
2 tablespoons butter
¼ teaspoon ground ginger
1 teaspoon turmeric (optional)

2 tomatoes, cut in wedges
2 potatoes, cut in quarters
1 tablespoon lemon juice
2 teaspoons curry powder
Pinch salt

1 String the beans and cut into 2.5 cm (1 in.) pieces.

2 Heat butter in frying pan and fry onions and ginger until onions are a light golden brown.

3 Add turmeric and salt and fry 2 to 3 minutes.

4 Add tomatoes.

5 Mix well and cook until most of the liquid has evaporated.

6 Add beans and potatoes.

7 Mix well, cover, and cook until beans and potatoes are tender.

8 Add lemon juice and curry powder about 5 minutes before food is removed from heat.

This curry should be dry. Makes about 4 servings.

If you were to cook this bean curry in an Indian village you would probably cook it over a fire, because most homes in Indian villages do not have gas or electric stoves. Girls and women carry the water they need in brass pots from the village well for cooking and sometimes for bathing. These brass pots are an important household item even in houses that have running water, because they are used for storing food and pouring water.

Bharat Guides

In India, girls ages 6 to 10 are Bulbuls (Bluebirds). Girls ages 11 to 17 are Guides. Girls over 17 are Rangers. They all belong to the Bharat Guides. Bharat is an ancient name for India.

Bulbuls meet in a group called a flock. Flock leaders are usually teachers in the school where the Bulbuls meet. Like Bulbul flocks, Guide companies and Ranger teams meet in the schools which the Guides attend. In most parts of India, Girl Guiding is like a school club.

To learn how to obey the Guide Law, girls are asked to name women from Indian history whose lives fulfill the Law. They are also expected to think of ways to carry out the Law in daily life. One of the Guide Laws says, "A Guide's duty is to revere God, serve her country, and help others."

For example, if a Guide lives in a village, she must know what crops are grown and where and when the village *panchayat* (council) meets. Guides in cities and villages must be able to direct a stranger to the nearest doctor; to fire, police, and railway stations; as well as to post and telegraph offices. In India the telegraph is important because there are not many telephones. People send telegrams when they need to communicate quickly.

Older Guides and Rangers also help teach women about nutrition and child care. Rangers are

introducing Girl Guiding to girls who have left school or have never attended school. Flocks and companies are being started in community centers and in remote farming villages. Rangers also help older women in villages to read who have never been to school.

Hiking and trekking are favorite activities of the Bharat Guides. They especially enjoy singing and like to learn songs in the many languages of India.

India is the home of Sangam, one of our world centers. Look at the introduction to this book to find out what Girl Guides and Girl Scouts from all over the world can do while visiting Sangam.

Pratigya

Main maryada purvak pratigya
karti hoon ki yathashakti Ishwar
aur apne desh ke prati apne
kartavya kā pālan karungi.
Sada dusron ki sahayata karungi.
Guide Niyamon kā pālan karungi.

Promise

On my honor I promise that I will do my best:
To do my duty to God and my country;
To help other people at all times;
To obey the Guide Law.

Uniforms
Blue dress
Light blue tie
Or
White dress and pants
Blue sash
Red tie
Girl Guide Pin
Green trefoil with gold outline

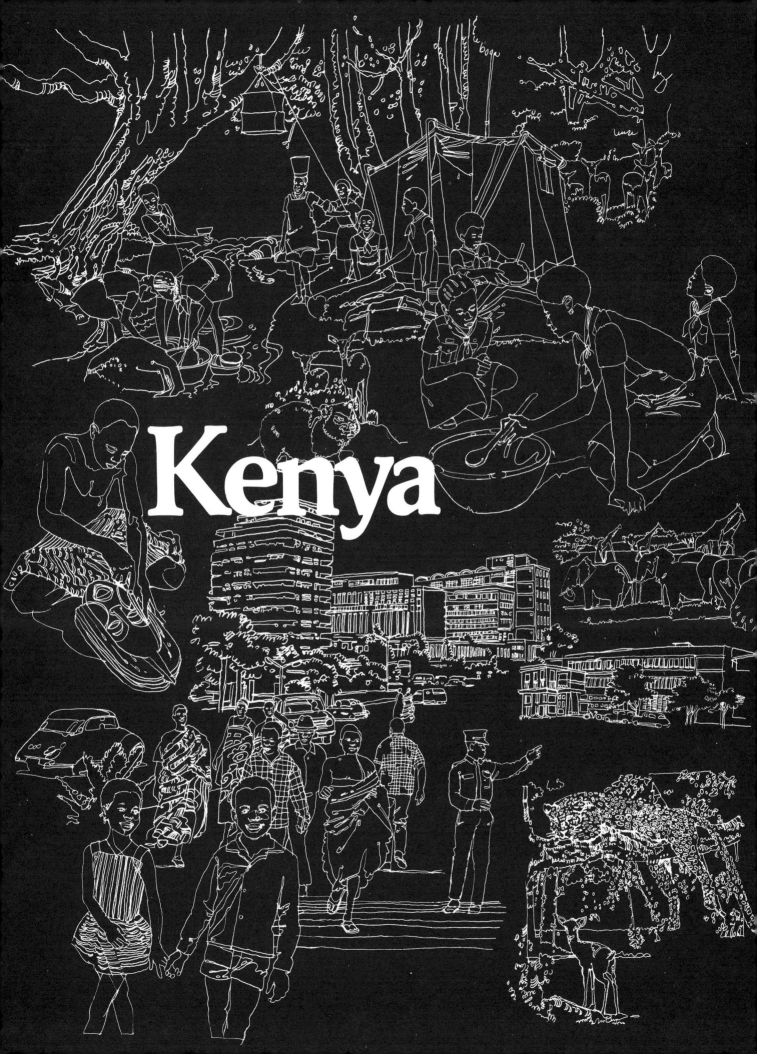

Can you imagine grown-ups who spend all their time digging? These men and women, who are called archaeologists, are seeking to uncover whatever has been buried beneath the earth for centuries upon centuries. In doing so, they have unlocked many secrets of the beginnings of life on earth.

Africa is often described as the birthplace of the human race and the cradle of human civilization. And Kenya, sometimes called the "Hawaii of Africa," is the specific area where the earliest human life on earth was discovered!

Kenya sits on the east coast of Africa facing the Indian Ocean and is about the size of Texas. Along the coast, the country is wet and tropical. Many Kenyans live in Nairobi, the sophisticated capital city, or in the rich, lush countryside nearby. Farming is the way of life for most of the people in this area; coffee, tea, fruits, and vegetables are grown and sold to other countries. Mt. Kenya, which is very near the equator, is one of the highest mountains in the world; it has 12 glaciers on its summit.

If you were going down the highway from Nairobi to Mombasa (one of Kenya's oldest cities), you would see signs saying: Warning — Elephants Have Right of Way. Kenya is one of the best places in the world to see large animals. Kenya's game parks and reserves cover enormous areas of land. The land of many of the game parks is called a savanna and looks much like the Great Plains of the United States. As people have needed more land for their homes and farms, the animals of the savanna have moved farther and farther away.

Generally, the parks are without fences, so the animals can migrate if they need more water or food. From one of the parks, you can see the skyscrapers of Nairobi. This park does have a fence on the side facing Nairobi, but the animals are free to wander out on any other side.

Kenya's official language is English, but Swahili is the widely spoken second language. Because Swahili developed as a trade language between East Africans and Arab traders, it has many Arabic words. The majority of the Kenyan people speak this Bantu language. You may already know some words in Swahili: *simba* (lion), *uhuru* (freedom), and *harambee* (let's all pull together). You might enjoy learning more words on the *Say It In Another Language* cassette, like *jambo* (hello), *kwaheri* (good-bye), and *harbari ganı* (how are you?).

Let's take a safari! In Swahili and in English, that means taking a journey.

Try constructing a scene you might see on safari. First, prepare the habitat which is right for the animals you want to show. Then add the animals. You might want to do your scene as a mural and construct your animals out of paper. They could be small or large, and could have backing so they stand out. Instead of paper, you might prefer to work in stitchery or felt and design a tapestry. Use magazines and books to give you ideas for the vegetation and the variety of animals that are found in Kenya.

Kenya is made up of several groups of people. These groups are different from each other in many ways. The Kikuyu and Luo have had an important part in the government, because they have the greatest number of people. Two other large groups are the Kamba and Masai, who live in the areas near the big game animals. The Kamba are well known for their fine wood carvings of people and animals. The Masai were known to be great warriors.

Over the years, Kenya has seen many kinds of people come and go within its borders. Arab traders explored Kenya as early as the 8th century, and other peoples sought the wealth hidden in natural resources of the land. Europeans came to Kenya in the 15th century, beginning with the Portuguese. Many years later the British came and, from 1920 to 1961, Kenya was a colony of Great Britain. In 1961, Kenya achieved independence. Each year on December 12, Kenyans celebrate their independence just as we celebrate ours on July 4. Jomo Kenyatta, a great Kikuyu leader, was important in helping Kenya achieve independence. He was president of Kenya from the time of independence until his death in 1978.

Kenya has been important to Girl Guiding for many years. This nation is the burial place of Lord Baden-Powell, the man who started Boy Scouting, and his wife, Lady Baden-Powell, who was our World Chief Guide for 47 years.

One of the favorite spots of the Baden-Powells was Nyeri near Mt. Kenya. Their home there was Paxtu, a Swahili word meaning "complete." Lord Baden-Powell spent his final years at Nyeri enjoying the flowers, the bright colored birds, and the abundant wildlife. He even made pets of two rock hyrax.

The Baden-Powells loved to visit Treetops, a famous lodge near Paxtu. They would spend the night there watching the many animals that came to drink at the pools below. Treetops, as its name indicates, is a house built in a tree and is a perfect spot for seeing animals. The Kenyan Girl Guides are very proud that a place in their country was so well loved by the Baden-Powells.

Kenya Girl Guides Association

In Kenya, girls ages 8 to 11 are Brownies, ages 11 to 15 are Guides, and ages 16 to 21 are Rangers.

Camping is important in Kenya just as it is in the United States. The Kenyan Guides usually make their own campsites, so they must be very careful about the environment and the local wildlife.

For instance, food is stored in hanging larders out of the reach of little animals. Also, the Guides choose their sites so they do not interfere with the animals' territory or sources of food and water. If there are crocodiles in a nearby river, swimming is out of the question! Camping outdoors near the wildlife

helps Girl Guides to understand better the habits and needs of animals.

People are concerned that most of the animals in Kenya will be gone soon. Many animals which once wandered the savannas, highlands, and jungles of East Africa are now extinct. Kenyan Girl Guides learn about their government's laws against hunting and the export of animal skins and other animal products. Guides are working with the United Nations in Kenya on ways to help the people and save the environment.

The Girl Guides take first aid training. They help people where there are no doctors or nurses, as well as take care of themselves at camp.

The younger Guides combine what they know about knot tying and wildlife into a fun game. They call it Home of the Dik-Dik. One girl is a mama dik-dik and one girl is a leopard. The other girls are the baby dik-diks, and they each have a length of rope. When mama dik-dik sees the leopard approach, she claps her hands. The baby dik-diks form a circle by tying their rope into a ring around themselves to make the "home of the dik-dik." They should all use the same kind of knot. The leopard inspects the knots and "eats up" any baby dik-dik who has tied the wrong knot.

You can make up your own game like this one. Decide how to choose someone to be mama dik-dik

and the leopard, what knot the baby dik-diks will tie, and what happens to the baby dik-diks the leopard "eats up."

Another special interest for Girl Guides in Kenya is nutrition. They learn how to plan menus and how to teach others about eating the right foods. Guide companies (troops) often have their own gardens on their school grounds where they raise vegetables and fruit. The Girl Guides of Kenya have their own cookbook which has favorite Kenyan recipes. Some of the ingredients used frequently in the recipes are maize (corn), sweet potatoes, bananas, dried beans, nuts, and rice. A few of the recipes use curry, which shows the influence of the Asians from India and Pakistan living in Kenya. Here is one of the recipes from the Kenyan cookbook, *Let Us Cook the Girl Guides' Way*.

Stuffed Baked Sweet Potatoes

6 sweet potatoes
½ cup nuts
2 tablespoons milk
3 tablespoons butter or margarine
Salt and pepper to taste

1 Wash potatoes and boil them until soft.

2 Cut potatoes along one side and remove the inside. Be careful not to break the skins. Mash potatoes with milk, butter, salt, and pepper.

3 Mix in nuts which have been pounded into a fine paste.

4 Fill the skins with the mixture, and bake at 350 degrees F for 30 minutes. Serve hot.

Cheese, chopped hard-boiled egg, or mashed dried beans can be used instead of nuts. Use one tablespoon each per potato. Makes 6 servings.

Promise

I promise on my honor that I will do my best:
To do my duty to God and my Country,
To help other people at all times,
And to obey the Guide Law.

English is the language used by the Girl
Guides of Kenya, so they use that language
for their Promise.

Uniform
Dark blue dress
Red tie
Girl Guide Pin
Gold trefoil
Brownie Pin
Gold bird on tan tie ring

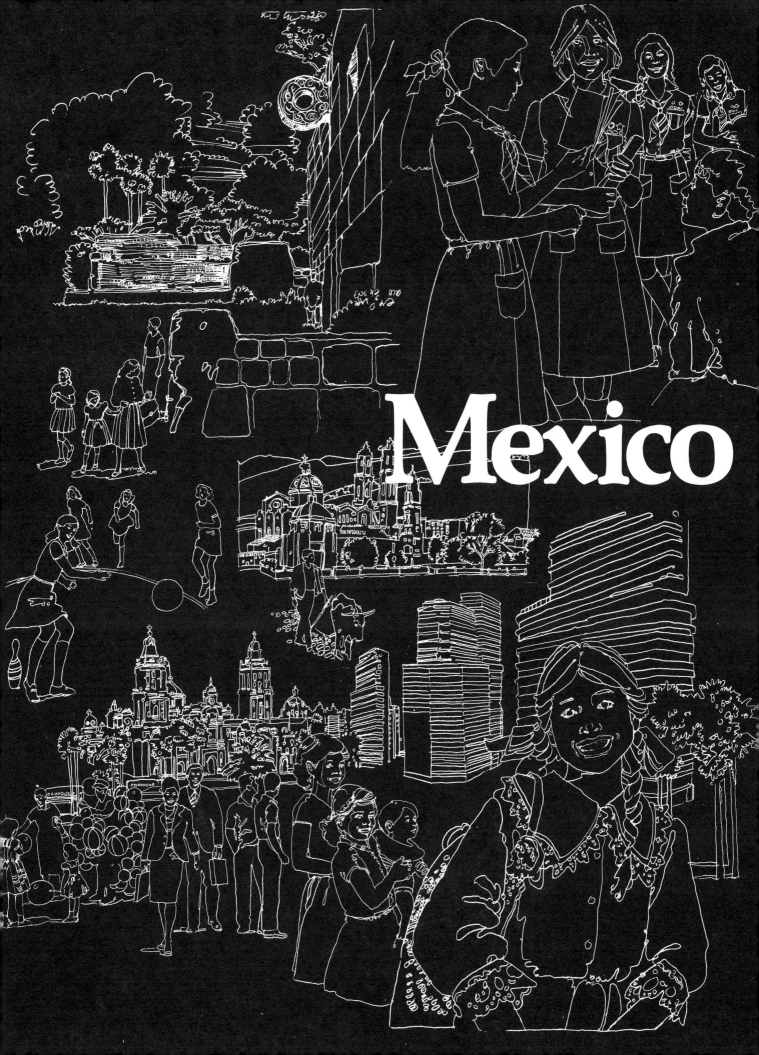

Mexico

Mexico is often called our neighbor, because this nation is right next door. If you live along the southwest border of the United States, you may have visited Mexico. Remains of the Mexican Indian civilizations, including their giant pyramids, can be found in many parts of Mexico. As interesting to see are the quiet country towns with cobblestone streets and high-walled buildings hiding lovely courtyards.

The most important center is Mexico City, the oldest and largest city in the Western Hemisphere. Mexico City, the capital of the United States of Mexico, is on a high plateau which was once a lake. It is a very

large, busy city. Because of its climate and history, Mexico City looks much like cities in California or the southwestern states.

Children in Mexico play outside all year without heavy coats. From May to October, rain falls for a few hours each day. During the rest of the year, the sun shines every day.

The Spanish conquistadores, who came to the Southwest in 1545, more than 100 years before the Pilgrims landed in Massachusetts, went first to Mexico to search for gold and silver. At that time, a group of Aztec Indians named the Mexicas lived in what is now Mexico City. The Spanish conquered the Aztec Indians as they did many American Indians, from New Mexico through Central America all the way to Chile in South America.

The Spanish introduced their language wherever they went. Mexicans today speak Spanish, but still use some Indian words. You use some words of Mexican Indian origin: coyote, tomato, and chocolate. Some well-known Spanish place names in the United States are Los Angeles, the Rio Grande, and San Francisco.

Mexico has mountains, deserts, jungles, and coastlines. There are not many places where farming is easy, but still much lettuce and tomatoes come to us from Mexico. Fishing is also important. As more and more oil is being found in Mexico, the oil industry there is growing.

Mexicans enjoy sports as much, if not more, than North Americans. Over 1,000 years ago, the Maya and other Mexican Indians built handsome ball courts in their cities. One of the games they played was a little like basketball and soccer. The players had to knock the ball through a high ring using their elbows, wrists, or hips, but not their hands. Today, Mexicans play baseball, basketball, jai alai, and soccer.

To play a game somewhat like the Mayan ball game, you might try Soccer Guard. You will need:

- A soccer ball, or any ball the size of a volleyball that is hard enough to kick
- A goal, which can be an unbreakable container or a bowling pin

Make a single circle. Place the goal in the center of the circle. A guard stands near the goal, ready to protect it. The girls forming the circle try to knock over the goal by kicking the ball. The guard protects the goal by kicking the ball away from it. Whenever the goal is knocked over, the girl who kicked the ball changes places with the guard. If the guard accidentally knocks over the goal, she must change places with someone who has not had a chance to guard.

The ball should be kept low and may not be thrown. Girls may touch the ball with their hands only to protect themselves from a ball kicked too high. To make the game faster, use two goals and two guards within the circle.

Many Mexican hand arts reflect the Indian and Spanish heritage of the people. You may have tried the *Ojo de Dios*, or Eye of God, made with two crossed sticks and yarn. Another art form created by the Huichol Indians is the *nearika*, a painting made of yarn. The original yarn paintings were religious. Now they are also made for decoration. To make a *nearika*, you will need:

- 2 to 3 ounces 3-ply yarn in 3 or 4 colors. Use 3 mm (⅛ in.) diameter yarn.
- Smooth, flat piece of wood, 21.5 cm x 28 cm (8½ in. x 11 in.)
- White glue

step 1.

1 Spread glue in one small area of the wood base at a time so that it will not dry out. Cut a piece of yarn for the outside edge and twist the end. Press down the yarn with the thumbnail, all around the outside edge of the board. Press a second row close to the first. Hold yarn tightly with one hand while you position with the other. Turns must be sharp and definite — never let the yarn twist or overlap. Place the third row close inside the second. Most traditional *nearikas* have three colors bordering the edge.

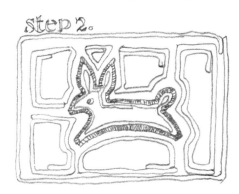

step 2.

2 Place glue for the outline of the central figure. Press down a row of yarn. Put a second row inside this. Then a third, fourth, and fifth row, until the body is filled almost to the center. Often, a second color is added in the center section of the body. You could also outline the animal (or whatever you design) in one color and fill in with another. When the figure is complete, cut yarn, twist end, and press. Next, fill in any additional figures.

step 3.

3 The last step is doing the background. Fill in open areas with one continuous strand until you can no longer fit in the yarn. Then start a new area. These areas will depend on your design. No two *nearikas* are ever alike. The small areas require more patience and pressing with the thumbnail. When all yarn is pressed in place, your *nearika* is complete.

Guías de Mexico

Girl Guides in Mexico are known as Guías. Girls ages 6 to 10 are Haditas, ages 10 to 13 are Guías Intermedias, ages 13 to 15 are Guías, and ages 15 to 18 are Guías Mayores.

One of the Guías' Laws says, *El deber de una Guía es ser útil y ayudar a los demás* (A Guide's duty is to be useful and help all others). To do this, a Guía might try the Farm Worker's badge, so that she can help on a farm. Here are some of the badge requirements:

1 Help plant or harvest for at least a week.

2 Know how to milk a cow.

3 Know how to ride a horse, Western and English style.

4 Know the names and uses of farm tools.

5 Know how to feed farm animals.

6 Have an idea of how to prevent sickness in animals.

7 Know the daily routine of a farm.

Physical fitness is an important part of the Guías' program. During meetings, Haditas might try somersaults, or carry books on their heads for 10 m (11 yds.). In order to earn the Sportswoman's badge, some of the things a Guía must do are run 100 m (108 yds.) in 28 seconds, jump over a 90 cm (1 yd.) hurdle, and skip rope 30 times in a row. You can try some of these, too.

Older Guías help in a Literacy Center near Mexico City. This is a school for children whose families have come from rural areas. It is not easy for these families to find work, a new place to live, and adapt to city life. Sometimes, it is difficult for them to send their children to school. The Guías' school is for these children.

Mexico is the home of one of our world centers. There is information about Our Cabaña in the introduction to this book. Did you know that Mexico also has a special building named Ticalli in Mexico City? *Ticalli* is a Mexican Indian word which means "your house," and it is the headquarters for Guías de Mexico. It also has dormitory space, a breakfast room, and meeting rooms for Girl Guides/Girl Scouts visiting Mexico City from Mexico or any other country.

Promesa

Yo prometo por mi honor hacer cuanto de mi dependa para:

Cumplir con mi deber hacia Dios y mi Patria;

Ser útil al prójimo en todas las circunstancias,

Y obedecer la Ley Guía.

Promise

I promise on my honor to do my best:

To do my duty to God and my Country;

To help other people in all circumstances,

And to obey the Guide Law.

Uniform
White shirt
Grey skirt
Purple tie

Girl Guide Pin
Gold trefoil

Hadita Pin
Gold Brownie

Peru

Traveling through different parts of Peru, you might see jets, buses, trains, cars, trucks, llamas, steamships, and canoes transporting people and equipment. In cities, you can see modern apartments and office buildings standing next to Spanish houses with their lovely wooden balconies and courtyards. You'd also see snow-capped mountains, deserts, jungles, farms, and ocean beaches.

Peru is well known for its ancient Indian civilizations and the great Inca cities high in the Andes Mountains. These majestic cities, built of enormous stones which fit together without cement, were constructed 300 to 700 years ago.

The buildings were so well made that they have not been disturbed by great earthquakes. Some Spanish and modern buildings have been constructed on these Inca foundations. Today, descendants of the Incas still live in Peru, and some of them in the mountain villages even use the same tools and dress that their ancestors used.

Recently, interesting evidence of Indians who lived in Peru many years before the Incas was found. In the Nazca Desert, the driest in the world, giant drawings of animals, birds, and straight lines made about 2,000 years ago were discovered. The amazing thing is that these drawings cannot be seen very well from the ground, only from a tower or a low-flying airplane.

A little more than 150 years ago, Peru declared its independence from Spain. Peru celebrates its independence each year on July 28 and 29. In some cities, the fiestas and festivals last for a whole week.

Many people in the villages of Peru use a drop spindle to spin yarn from sheep and alpaca fibers the same way they have done for hundreds of years. A drop spindle is a smooth stick with a weight, or whorl, near one end around which the spun yarn winds as the spindle turns.

You can make an "instant" drop spindle by sticking a 40 cm (16 in.) dowel through the center of an apple. There will probably not be a llama or alpaca nearby as a source of fiber, but you can try making yarn from cotton batting.

Llamas and alpacas are members of the camel family. You can tell alpacas from llamas by their ears. The alpacas' ears stand up and forward. The llamas' ears lie back. The llama was domesticated by the Incas as a pack animal to carry heavy burdens along narrow mountain trails.

The alpaca is similar to the llama, but not as tall or as strong. The alpaca is raised for its long, soft hair. Alpaca wool is woven or knitted into beautiful, warm clothing and blankets.

Peruvians also make colorful belts of alpaca yarn by finger weaving. You can find out how to weave one in *Exploring the Hand Arts*, pages 93 and 94. Try your skill at creating a belt for yourself.

The Andean condor is a huge bird found in Peru. It has great wings that open to 2.6 to 3 m (8½ to 10 ft.), and it can fly as high as 6,100 m (20,000 ft.). The condor hunts for other animals to eat. It has sharp talons (claws) so it can tear meat apart. Because the condor is becoming extinct, this bird is protected by law.

The Guías in Peru have a favorite game called The Condor and the Chicks. To play, divide the group into teams of 6 to 8 girls. Pick one girl out of each team to be a condor. The other girls line up in a single line. Each girl holds on to the girl in front of her. The girl in the front of each line is the hen. She must protect her chicks from the condor. The condor in each team tries to grab a chick out of her line. The hen tries to keep her from doing this by using her outstretched arms between the condor and the chick. If the line breaks or the condor grabs a chick out of the line before the signal is given to stop, the condor changes place with the hen, who then becomes a condor (or the hen may want to choose a chick to be the condor).

Peru

Hundreds of years ago the Indians in the Andes Mountains used freeze-drying to preserve their food. Freeze-dried foods are found today in some of the village markets of Peru. Freeze-drying out-of-doors takes a

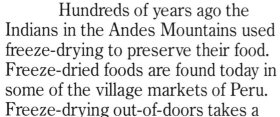

the same time the food is dried by the sun. Sometimes winds help the process. When these foods are soaked for a short time in water, they are ready to be eaten or used in cooking. Today, backpackers use freeze-dried foods to cut down on the weight they carry. You may have eaten commercially freeze-dried foods in your own home.

Potatoes, peanuts, gourds, pumpkins, lima beans, and corn are a few of the foods grown by people in Peru and sold in their markets. When the Spaniards conquered Peru, they took two new plants — peanuts and potatoes — home with them. From Spain, these plants spread to Africa, to Asia, to Europe, and then on to the North American colonies.

special climate with cold, windy air and bright sun. The food is placed outside at night so the water in it will freeze. During the day, the bright sun evaporates the water as it melts. At

Guías del Perú

In Peru, Girl Guides are known as Guías. Girls ages 7 to 9 are Alitas, ages 10 to 13 are Guías Intermedias, and ages 14 to 18 are Guías Mayores. Young women ages 19 to 25 are Guías de Servicios. Girl Guiding has been honored by Peru's Ministry of Education for its outstanding community service.

As in many cities of the world, Peru's capital city, Lima, has been growing very rapidly, making it difficult for the Peruvian government to help all the people. The Guías help people who have moved to Lima from the mountains and rural areas. They hold classes to teach people how to read, write, and speak Spanish. They help families adjust to city life, and

operate day-care centers where working parents can leave small children. Some of the Guías have been working together with Swiss Girl Guides in a nutrition program in Peru.

Like many countries bordering on the Pacific Ocean, Peru has earthquakes. When they occur, the Guías show that they live up to their motto, *Estar Preparada* (Be Prepared). The Peruvian Ministry of Health knows it can count on the Guías to help. Guías also help with reforestation projects, and they plant shrubs and flowers which make their cities and countryside attractive.

Guías of all ages like outdoor activity. They go camping, play games, and learn about the different animals and plants of Peru. They may even hike along the ancient Inca roads and explore Machu Picchu, the most famous of the Inca cities.

When Guías of Peru go camping or have cookouts, they cook over charcoal or in a *pachamanca* (bean hole). A special dish of the Peruvian Guías is *causa*. It combines many of their favorite foods — tuna, potatoes, corn, avocados, eggs, and olives. One Guía called *causa* her favorite one-pot meal. Here is how to make *causa*.

Causa

Potato Mixture

6 medium potatoes, cooked
Juice of 5 lemons
½ cup salad oil
1 raw egg
1 teaspoon salt
½ teaspoon pepper
Paprika to taste

Filling

2 7-ounce cans tuna, drained
1 cup mayonnaise
1 cup cooked whole kernel corn (or 1 8-ounce can, drained)
2 avocados, chopped

Optional Toppings

Sliced hard-boiled eggs
Black olives
Queso Blanco, Mozzarella, or Muenster cheese, cut in chunks

1 Mash potatoes and mix with lemon juice, salad oil, egg, salt, pepper, and paprika.

2 Press half of mixture into well-oiled baking dish or shallow bowl.

3 Mix ingredients for filling and place on potato mixture.

4 Cover with remaining potato mixture, pressing to seal in filling.

5 Unmold on large serving dish.

6 Top with slices of hard-boiled eggs, black olives, and/or cheese chunks, if you wish.

Makes 8 servings.

Promesa

Prometo por mi honor, hacer todo lo posible,
Para cumplir mis deberes, para con Dios y mi Patria,
Ayudar a mis semejantes en todo momento,
Y obedecer la Ley Guía.

Promise

I promise on my honor, to do everything possible,
To accomplish my duties toward God and my Country,
To help all human beings at any time,
And to obey the Guide Law.

Uniform
White shirt
Dark blue skirt
Light blue tie
Girl Guide Pin
Silver trefoil on silver background
Alita Pin
Silver Brownie

Philippines

Tropical flowers; palm trees lining the ocean shore; steep mountains with rice terraces, deep canyons, and waterfalls — all this is part of the beauty of the Philippines. The capital city, Manila, is so lovely it is called the "Pearl of the Orient." Imagine living in a country which has 7,100 islands! Think of what it would be like to travel around your country or to visit relatives when it would mean going long distances between islands.

The Philippines are so near the equator that the weather is always very warm and ideal for growing tropical crops. Much of the sugar used in the United States comes from the sugarcane in the Philippines. Coconut trees are also grown on many farms. Coconut oil is used in soap, candy bars, and cattle feed. Mahogany trees grow in the mountain forests. The wood from these trees is made into beautiful furniture. Fishing is also important in this nation surrounded by the waters of the Pacific Ocean.

Christianity was introduced in the Philippines by the Spanish when Magellan arrived 500 years ago, and has been the major religion ever since. People from all over Asia have come to the Philippines to live, introducing many different religions and cultures. Arab traders from the Middle East brought the Muslim religion, which many people living in the southern islands of the Philippines still follow.

Philippines

A dance popular in the Philippines, which has spread to many parts of the world, is the Tinikling or the Bamboo Poles Dance. The dance imitates the movements of the tickling bird as it hops in and out of the thick undergrowth so its feet won't get caught. For this dance, you will need:

- 2 bamboo poles or broomstick handles, each about 3 m (10 ft.) long
- 2 wooden crossbars, each 5 cm x 75 cm (2 in. x 30 in.)

Two people, called clappers, kneel on each end of the bamboo poles. They slap the poles together twice, then slide them about 38 cm (15 in.) from the center of the crossbars and hit them twice against the bars in a rhythm like this—tap, tap, slide; tap, tap, slide. The clappers should not lift the poles because the dancers' feet could easily get caught in them. You can learn or make up many steps to dance in and out of the poles.

Two dancers stand outside on the same side of the bamboo poles. The dancers face each other, so that when one uses the right foot the other uses the left foot as they move in the same direction.

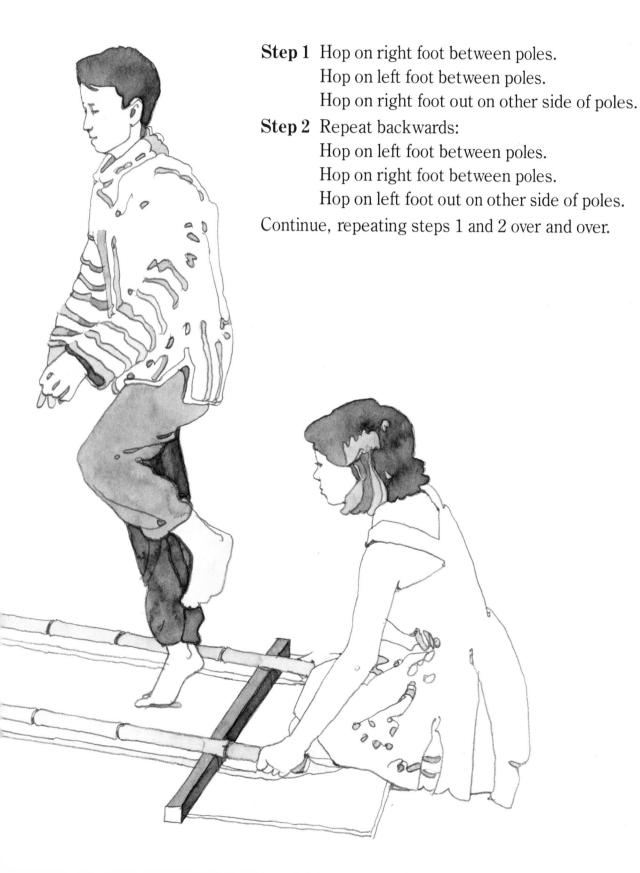

Step 1 Hop on right foot between poles.
Hop on left foot between poles.
Hop on right foot out on other side of poles.

Step 2 Repeat backwards:
Hop on left foot between poles.
Hop on right foot between poles.
Hop on left foot out on other side of poles.

Continue, repeating steps 1 and 2 over and over.

Philippines

In the Philippines and many islands of the Pacific, outrigger canoes have been used for fishing, transportation, and sport for centuries. Families travel between islands on their outriggers, and even the mail is transported this way to more remote areas. Small boats are needed to go in shallow waters near the islands and coral reefs. That's why the Filipinos use canoes. Since these boats must also travel on the ocean, the outrigger is added to balance the canoe in rough waters. Some of the outriggers in the Philippines which have sails are called *vintas*.

You might like to make an outrigger. With other girls in your troop, you could have a gam. A gam is a gathering of boats. For your outrigger, you will need:

- A quart-size milk carton (makes 2 hulls)
- 2 sticks for crosspieces, each 26 cm (10 in.) long
- 2 sticks for pontoons, each 23 cm (9 in.) long
- String to lash sticks together and use for painter (bow rope)

1 Cut off top of milk carton.

2 Cut carton in half down the opposite seams.

3 Cut off bottom of carton.

4 Trim top sides of carton so hull is 4 to 5 cm (2 in.) high.

5 To form bow (front) and stern (back), cut corners off and tape closed with masking tape.

6 Cut two holes in hull—one near the bow and one near the stern, each 1 cm (½ in.) from bottom.

7 Take the two crosspieces and put one crosswise to the hull in each hole.

8 Square lash pontoons under the crosspieces, so they are parallel to hull and will keep the outrigger afloat in the water. (See pages 376 and 377 of *Worlds to Explore* for more information about square lashing.)

9 Make a small hole near the top of the bow. Put string at least 15 cm (6 in.) long through hole and tie a bowline knot. This string may be used as a painter to tie up your outrigger or pull it through the water.

10 If you like, you can decorate or cover the hull with contact paper. You may want to add a mast and sail. For long trips, outriggers equipped with a sail like the *vinta* pictured are used.

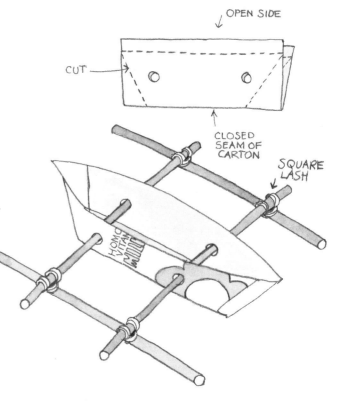

OPEN SIDE

CUT

CLOSED SEAM OF CARTON

SQUARE LASH

Girl Scouts of the Philippines

There are five age levels in the Philippine Girl Scouts: Twinklers, ages 4 to 6; Star Scouts, ages 6 to 9; Junior Scouts, ages 9 to 12; Senior Scouts, ages 13 to 15; and Cadets, ages 15 to 18.

The name Star was chosen because stars are beautiful, provide light, and give direction to boats. The Star Scouts have three songs of their own. One is "The Star Scout Smile Song," and you would recognize it right away. It begins, "I've something in my pocket...." Here's another short song of theirs you might enjoy singing.

The Star Scouts' Song

We're the Star Scouts, Here's our aim Lend a hand and play the game.

Where the Star Scouts live and play   That is where we love to stay.

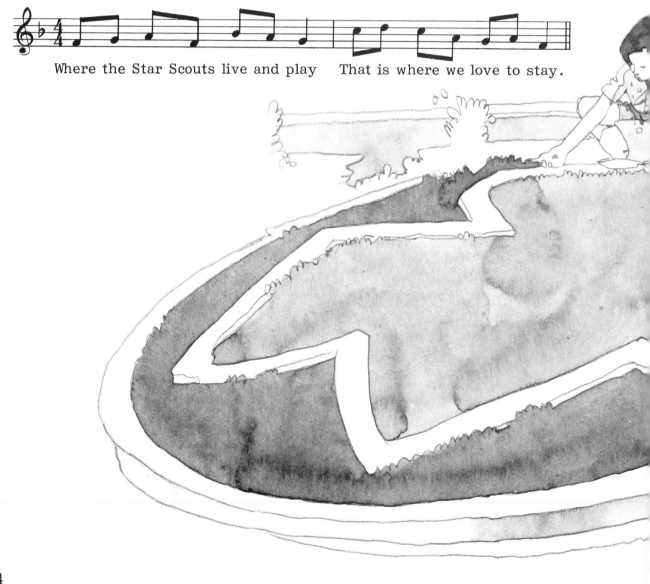

Girl Scouts in the Philippines help their country through several projects. One is a Greening Project, which includes planting trees or flowering bushes on Thinking Day and making "magic spots" or mini-parks in crowded city areas. They have planted gardens in the shape of trefoils to brighten up school yards, public parks, and vacant lots. From these projects, they have become skilled at gardening. The Girl Scouts are growing food in areas where it is needed and sharing what they know about gardening with others.

Emergency Preparedness is another important project in a country where there are earthquakes, typhoons, and active volcanoes. Girl Scouts are trained to take care of children and give first aid when disaster strikes so that adults can help where they are needed. Afterward, Girl Scouts are often involved in reforestation projects to prevent harmful erosion from floods in the lowlands.

Girl Scouts of all ages have fun preserving their Filipino heritage. Some belong to troops who perform at cultural events. Others sponsor talent shows of traditional music, songs, and dances. They have also organized a nationwide radio/TV Girl Scout club, which gives broadcasts. Girl Scout theater guilds encourage the talents of every Girl Scout.

Special activities such as weekend festivals bring together Girl Scouts of the Philippines with TOFS (Troops on Foreign Soil). These are Girl Scouts from the United States who live with their families outside the United States.

Pangako

Sa aking karangalan, gagampanan ko
ang aking tungkuling maglingkod sa Diyos,
Sa aking bayan at sa sangkatauhan at
mananatiling tapat sa Batas ng Girl Scout.

The Promise is in Tagalog, the common
language of the Philippines.

Promise

On my honor, I will fulfill my duty:
To serve God,
My country and mankind,
And to abide by the Girl Scout Law.

Uniform
Green dress with trefoil print
Yellow tie

Girl Scout Pin
Gold trefoil with chevron; red on the right,
blue on the left, white on top with yellow sun

Star Scout Pin
Silver trefoil

Alicia I. Pagano, Ed.D., *Director*
Program Department/Educational Services

Carol N. Green, *Project Director*

Authors/Contributors
Janey Cole, Lucy Dinnes, Mabel A. Hammersmith,
Jean Hoff, Corinne M. Murphy, Lynn M. Obee

Kaaren Shandroff, *Illustrator*